SCIENCE Y5 / P6

Teacher's Notes
Changing State

James Driver

Series editor | Sue Palmer

Contents

	Page
What is Oxford Connections?	3
Page-by-page science and literacy notes	6
Pupils' book pages 2–3, 4–5	6
Pupils' book pages 6–7, 8–9	7
Pupils' book pages 10–11, 12–13	8
Pupils' book pages 14–15, 16–17	9
Pupils' book pages 18–19, 20–21	10
Pupils' book pages 22–23, 24–25	11
Pupils' book pages 26–27, 28–29	12
Pupils' book pages 30–31, 32–33	13
Pupils' book pages 34–35, 36–37	14
Pupils' book pages 38–39, 40–41	15
Pupils' book pages 42–43, 44–45	16
Pupils' book pages 46, 47–48	17
Step-by-step instructions on non-fiction text types	18
Recount	18
Instruction	24
Report	30
Explanation	36
Persuasion	42
Literacy (NLS) and Science (QCA) objectives	48

OXFORD
UNIVERSITY PRESS

Great Clarendon Street, Oxford OX2 6DP

Oxford University Press is a department of the University of Oxford.
It furthers the University's objective of excellence in research, scholarship,
and education by publishing worldwide in

Oxford   New York

Auckland Cape Town Dar es Salaam Hong Kong Karachi
Kuala Lumpur Madrid Melbourne Mexico City Nairobi
New Delhi Shanghai Taipei Tornoto

With offices in

Argentina Austria Brazil Chile Czech Republic France Greece
Guatemala Hungary Italy Japan Poland Portugal Singapore
South Korea Switzerland Thailand Turkey Ukraine Vietnam

Oxford is a registered trade mark of Oxford University Press
in the UK and in certain other countries

© James Driver 2003

The moral rights of the author have been asserted

Database right Oxford University Press (maker)

First published 2003

All rights reserved. No part of this publication may be reproduced,
stored in a retrieval system, or transmitted, in any form or by any means,
without the prior permission in writing of Oxford University Press,
or as expressly permitted by law, or under terms agreed with the appropriate
reprographics rights organization. Enquiries concerning reproduction
outside the scope of the above should be sent to the Rights Department,
Oxford University Press, at the address above

You must not circulate this book in any other binding or cover
and you must impose this same condition on any acquirer

British Library Cataloguing in Publication Data

Data available

ISBN-13: 978-0-19-834872-6
ISBN-10: 0-19-834872-X

9 10

Typeset by Fakenham Photosetting, Fakenham, Norfolk

Printed in the UK

What is Oxford Connections?

Oxford Connections is a set of 12 cross-curricular books and related teaching materials for 7 to 11 year olds. The books will help you teach literacy through a science, geography or history-based topic. Each book provides the material to cover one unit from the QCA Schemes of Work for the National Curriculum in England and Wales, and the non-fiction literacy objectives for one whole year of the National Literacy Strategy. (You can find a grid of where the QCA and NLS objectives are covered on p 48 of these notes and on the inside back cover of the pupils' books.) The books can be used to focus primarily on literacy or on science/geography/history.

Literacy

Pupils need different literacies. As well as traditional texts with different purposes and audiences, they also need to be able to understand and write material presented in different forms such as diagrams, bullet points, notes and Internet displays, particularly when working with non-fiction.

Oxford Connections supports the development of these different literacies. It focuses particularly on reading and writing non-fiction, and will help pupils use effectively the different non-fiction text types (report, explanation, instructions, recount, discussion, persuasion).

Using these books will help pupils to focus on the two main elements which make a text type what it is:

◆ the language features used (for example, present tense for instructions, and past tense for recounts, use of commands in instructions etc.).
◆ the structure of the text (for example, chronological order, in the case of instructions or recounts).

The structure of a text can be represented as a diagram or framework, showing visually how the parts of the text fit together, which are the main points and how they are developed etc. (A very common example of this type of presentation is a timeline, which shows events which have happened in the past, as a continuum, the order of which cannot change.) In this book, we refer to material presented in this diagrammatic way as *visual* (*visual reports, visual explanations* etc.).

Pupils will learn to read and to present information visually (by using frameworks) thus developing good note-taking skills, and consolidating their understanding of how texts are structured. The visual texts in particular are accessible to those pupils who need more support. Using frameworks to plan their own writing will also help improve all pupils' planning and drafting/editing skills.

In this book, we have used icons to represent the different sorts of frameworks you can use, called *skeletons*. These are referred to in the *National Literacy Strategy Support Materials for Text Level Objectives* (DfES 0532/2001). They can be used as an aide-memoir to help pupils remember the structures of each text type. They appear on pp 6–47 to show you what text types are on the pupils' book pages.

Recount	⊢⊢⊢→	Explanation	○→○→○
Instructions	○→○→○→	Persuasion	*≤ *≤ *≤
Non-chronological report	(cluster diagram)	Discussion	*|* *|* *|*

Using *Changing State* to teach literacy

There are step-by-step instructions to teach pupils how to read and write the different text types on pp 18–47 (a six-page section for each text type). They follow this model:

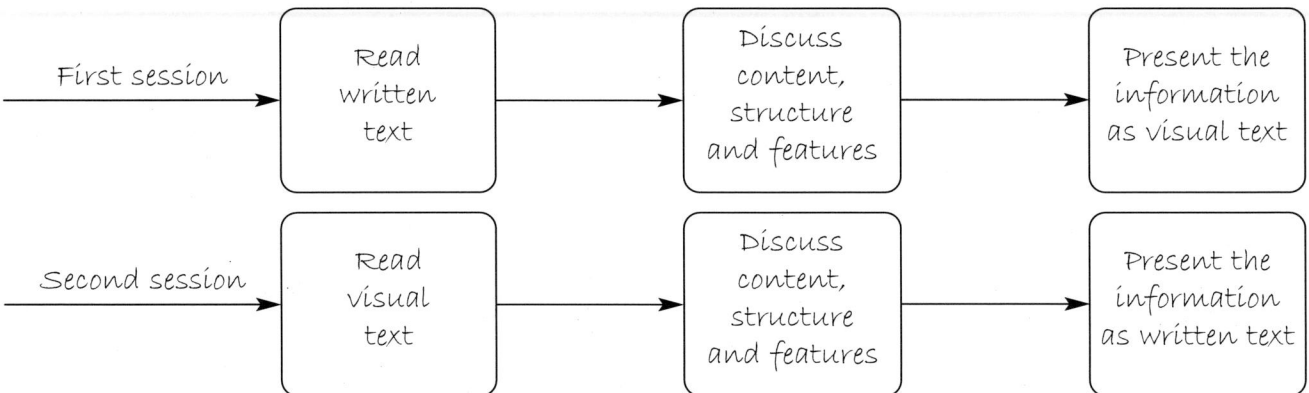

Each six-page section contains:

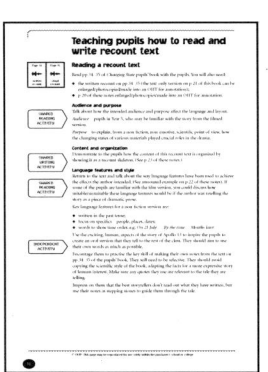 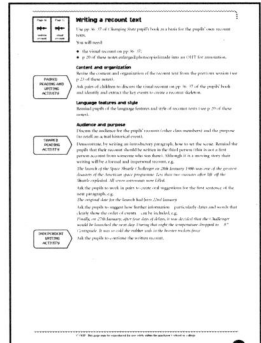 Two pages of step-by-step instructions taking you through the process described in the diagram above. They will help you analyse a written text, and then produce a visual version of that text with a group of children. You will then analyse a visual text, producing a written version.

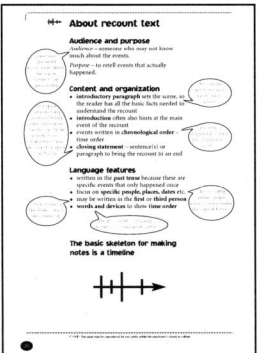 A page describing the relevant text type.*

 An example of the text type (an excerpt from *Changing State*) for you to read and analyse with children.*

 The same example with language features highlighted for your reference.*

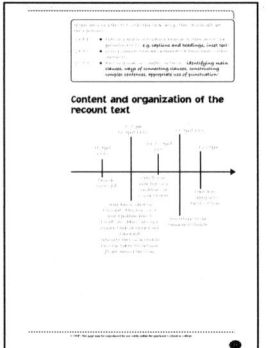 A visual version of the written text for your reference.*

*can be photocopied as handouts, a poster or an OHT

There are page-by-page notes on how to use the material to cover other aspects of literacy on pp 6–17. These page-by-page notes also show how to use the material in the pupils' book for the particular subject covered, e.g. science.

© OUP: This page may be reproduced for use solely within the purchaser's school or college

Speaking and listening, and drama

The discussion which is inherent in this method of learning should improve pupils' speaking and listening skills. As well as helping pupils to organize and structure their ideas before writing, visual texts should prompt pupils to use the relevant language features orally, as well as in writing. Additional speaking and listening, and drama activities such as those below, can be used to further reinforce the pupils' learning.

Retelling – events can be retold by an individual or by groups taking a section from a visual recount.

Role-play – using the visuals created by the whole class to ask/answer questions in role as the person in the recount or by taking one side of the argument etc.

Mini plays – retelling an event or following an explanation visual to show how something works. Pupils could be the different parts of whatever is being explained.

Puppet plays – retelling an event or following an explanation visual.

Freeze-frame – pupils in groups could show sections from a recount visual or report visual. They could show different aspects of a discussion.

TV/radio reports – demonstrating knowledge using a visual report as a TV/radio report. In a TV report images could be used either pictorially or by the use of freeze framing.

TV demonstrations – following an instruction visual or explanation visual to demonstrate making something or explaining how something works.

TV/radio interviews – retelling events in recounts or using report visuals while interviewing another pupil/pupils in role.

TV/radio adverts – using a persuasive visual to make adverts.

Illustrated talks – using the visual as a prompt.

Hot seat – answering questions in role – either as a persuasion, report or recount.

Debates – using discussion visuals to have debates between individuals or groups.

Using *Changing State* to teach Science

Changing State contains all the material you need to cover this topic, and to achieve the objectives of the *QCA Scheme of Work for the National Curriculum* Science Unit 5d (recommended for Year 5 pupils). There are page-by-page notes on how to use the material for science on pp 6–17. You can find a grid showing how the QCA objectives are covered on p 48 of these notes, and on the inside back cover of the *Changing State* pupils' book.

Which year group should I use *Changing State* with?

Changing State has been written for Year 5 pupils (9–10 year olds). However, if your school places the topic in another year group, the science material contained in *Changing State* will still be suitable for use with other age groups. Although all of the non-fiction literacy objectives for Year 5 are covered, many of the objectives for other year groups are also supported. Most of the six non-fiction text types are covered in it, and language features for Years 3, 4, and 6 are highlighted in the relevant sections.

SCOTLAND AND NORTHERN IRELAND

NB Throughout this introduction the term *Year 5* has been used to mean 9–10 year olds. The references in the grid on p 48 are to the *National Literacy Strategy* and to the *QCA Scheme of Work for the National Curriculum*. However, *Changing State* is suitable for use with P6 in Scotland and in Northern Ireland, since it supports many elements of the *National Guidelines, 5–14* and *The Northern Ireland Curriculum*. The science content of *Changing State* does not conflict in any way with either *National Guidelines, 5–14* or *The Northern Ireland Curriculum*.

Pages 2–3

Science

Use these pages as advance organizers to provide pupils with an overview of the work to be conducted:

concept map – shows the main areas to be covered and the links between them

contents page – shows how this information has been organized in the book.

- Use the introduction as an aid for using the contents page – ask the pupils to find what is being mentioned.
- Return to the pages occasionally during teaching to help the pupils see how their learning and understanding is building up.
- Use as a revision aid, asking pupils to summarize what they know about each aspect.
- Use the concept map at the end of the topic to review all areas of the topic covered.

Literacy

Help pupils to recognize the similarities and differences between the concept map and contents page:

- they contain the same information, but they are organized differently;
- the concept map provides an overview of the ideas contained in the book and how they are interlinked; the contents page provides a linear guide to the way these ideas are organized;
- the concept map and contents pages give page numbers for ease of reference.

Throughout your use of the book, demonstrate how to use the contents page – along with the index (see p 17 of these notes) – to access information when required.

Pages 4–5

Science

Key concepts

- Everything is made of matter.
- Matter is a general term for a variety of materials and substances.
- Matter takes three different forms: solid, liquid, gas.

Key vocabulary

- *materials, living things, solid, liquid, gas*

Suggested activities

- Discuss the different properties shown by the examples illustrated in the photograph at the top of p 4.
- Ask the pupils to make a list of *solids*, *liquids*, and *gases* that they encounter during their school day.
- Extend the pupils' investigations to include how changing state influences patterns and processes in geography. Can they, by using an atlas, find a pattern of where water, in its solid state as ice, is a predominate feature on the Earth's surface? Can they suggest how the process of melting ice at the poles might affect the quality of human lives?
- Ask them to investigate the power of water as a force for erosion in its solid state (e.g. as a glacier) and in its liquid state (e.g. as a fast flowing river or waterfall).

Literacy

Page 4	Page 5
written report	visual report

These pages are used as a featured example to teach pupils how to read and write **report** text. See pp 30–35 of these notes.

© OUP: This page may be reproduced for use solely within the purchaser's school or college

Pages 6–7

Science

Key concepts

- Single substances, e.g. water, can exist in different states.
- Different substances change state at different temperatures.
- Liquids can change to gases at different speeds, i.e. the evaporation of water speeds up as the temperature of the water rises.

Key vocabulary

- *cooling, heating, melting, evaporation, temperature*

Suggested activities

- Ask the pupils to note examples of everyday evaporation, e.g. puddles disappearing, wet footprints disappearing, clothes drying.
- Extend the pupils' investigative work by exploring how the changes in temperatures that might cause the icecaps to melt could be affected by an increase in global warming. Challenge them to come up with methods of limiting the emissions of gases produced by the burning of fossil fuels.

Literacy

Page 6	Page 7
written explanation	visual explanation

These pages are used as a featured example to teach pupils how to read and write **explanation** text. See pp 36–41 of these notes.

These pages also provide an opportunity to compare the advantages and disadvantages of visual and written explanations. They can help pupils to recognize that:

- visual explanations are more immediate than written versions;
- visual explanations often need written back-up, using technical vocabulary, to provide a more detailed understanding of complex ideas.

Pages 8–9

Science

Key concepts

- Scientific investigation relies on efficient, universally accepted methods of measurement to enable fair tests.
- Scientists develop instruments to keep pace with their investigations.

Key vocabulary

- *temperature, thermometer, scale, Fahrenheit, Celsius*

Suggested activity

- Using data from weather forecasts, in newspapers or on the Internet, explore how the daily temperature can be expressed on both Fahrenheit and Celsius scales.

Literacy

Page 8	Page 9
written explanation	written explanation

These pages combine historical recount with practical explanations of how temperature scales were developed. As the explanation relates to the past the usual present tense is replaced by the past tense. This is also why the usual impersonal, generalized style has been replaced with references to real people and individual events.

Challenge the pupils to reduce the written and visual information on p 8 down to a short section of notes by using the headings: What?, Why?, When?, How?, Where?, Who?, e.g. What? famous scientist; Why? gravity/telescope/thermometer; When? thermometer 1597; How? gravity: dropping cannonballs; Where? Italy/Pisa; Who? Galileo Galilei.

Discuss with them how they could use these notes: as memory prompts; the starting points for further research in the library or on the Internet; the key elements of the six paragraphs that might make up a biography of Galileo.

Pages 10–11

Science

Key concepts

- Visual summaries of the written explanations on pp 8–9.
- Scientific instruments can be made using a variety of techniques, e.g. three types of thermometer are listed here.

Key vocabulary

- *expand, contract, bulb, mercury, digital display*

Suggested activity

- Ask the pupils – or act as their scribe if you wish to use this as a shared session – to make comparisons between the three different types of thermometers by creating a grid. Down the left-hand side of the grid write the three different types of thermometer. Along the top create four columns for liquids, gases, solids, others. Ask the pupils to fill in the names of the materials, if any, that are employed by the different types of thermometers. For example:

	liquids	gases	solids	others
Galileo's	water	air	glass	–
Mercury	mercury	–	glass	–
Electronic	–	–	metal	electric current

Literacy

Page 10	Page 11
visual explanation	visual explanation

These pages are used as a featured example to teach pupils how to read and write **explanations**. See pp 36–41 of these notes.

Pages 12–13

Science

Key concepts

- Investigative skills can be practised using simple equipment.
- Comparisons can be made by changing one factor and observing or measuring the effect while keeping other factors the same.

Key vocabulary

- *thermometer, procedure, digital*

Suggested activities

- These pages contain instructions for using three different types of thermometer. In each case following the correct procedure is crucial to make fair tests. Divide the pupils into groups and, using one of the sets of instructions on p 13, ask them to repeat the same experiment, e.g. measuring the temperature of water in a beaker, then compare results and, if there are discrepancies, check that the instructions have been followed correctly. In both cases there is a necessity for a clear, progressive sequence of the important steps.
- Use these pages to remind pupils that an important part of science is the ability to test ideas using evidence from observation and measurement.

Literacy

Page 12	Page 13
written instructions	visual instructions

These pages are used as featured examples to teach pupils how to read and write **instructions**. See pp 24–29 of these notes.

Ask the pupils to turn the visual instructions for using the digital thermometer into a set of written instructions that follow the guidelines on p 26 of these notes.

© OUP: This page may be reproduced for use solely within the purchaser's school or college

Pages 14–15

Science

Key concepts
- Evaporation is when a liquid turns to a gas.
- Drying is an example of evaporation.
- Evaporation is affected by other conditions, e.g. temperature.
- Fair tests need controls to make them fair.

Key vocabulary
- *equipment, method, fair test, prediction, results, conclusion*

Suggested activities
- Using either graph paper or a spreadsheet with graph-making facilities, help the pupils to turn Table 1 into a simple visual representation of the results. (One axis will need to be a temperature range of 0 to 25°C, the other will need to range from 30 to 360 minutes.)
- When the graph is complete ask the pupils to use it to predict the likely drying time of a card placed in a room with a temperature of 15°C (about 160 minutes).

Literacy

Page 14	Page 15
‖‖‖→	‖‖‖→
written recount	visual recount

Ask the pupils to reduce the information contained in the recount of the experiments to 10 key bullet points, e.g.

- each card same size;
- each card tipped for 10 seconds;
- three different locations;
- no breeze.

These could then be used at a later date to create a set of instructions following the guidelines set out on p 20 of these notes.

The combination of the visual recount of results on p 15 accompanying the written recount on pp 14–15, offers pupils the opportunity to realize how a mass of information can be précised into a far simpler table.

Discuss with them which approach is the most useful for:

- scientific analysis;
- creating a model to follow in future investigations.

Pages 16–17

Science

Key concept
- Changes occur when materials are heated.

Key vocabulary
- *evaporation, water vapour, temperature*

Suggested activities
- p 16 explains how science can be related to everyday practical matters. The example given relates to drying clothes. Ask the pupils if they can use what they have learnt from this page to explain such everyday phenomena as:
  - nail varnish and correction fluid drying (the liquid has evaporated);
  - puddles vanishing when the sun shines (the water has changed state and evaporated not disappeared, it remains in the air as water vapour);
  - why perfume can be smelt from a distance (the liquid has evaporated but the gas carrying the scent has drifted to them through the air).
- Applying scientific knowledge can be used to solve problems, in this case drying clothes. Ask the pupils to brainstorm an initial list of everyday practical matters (e.g. non-pollutant transport, pencils that need sharpening) and then to follow them up with some scientific solutions.

Literacy

Page 16	Page 17
○→◊→	○→◊→
written explanation	visual explanation

Discuss whether it is easier to understand explanations through continuous text (p 16) or a labelled, visual representation. Ask the pupils to turn the explanation on how clothes dry on p 16 into a clear, concise, labelled diagram.

You might like to suggest to the pupils that they precede the exercise above by making a list of the three or four key points set out on p 16, for example:

Evaporation is speeded up by:
- warmth;
- greater surface area;
- moving not stationary air.

© OUP: This page may be reproduced for use solely within the purchaser's school or college

Pages 18–19

Science

Key concepts

- Evaporation is important when mammals need to keep cool.
- Humans sweat to keep cool.
- Elephants speed up the process by spraying themselves with water.
- Evaporation can be used to keep other things cool, too.

Key vocabulary

- *cooling, cooler, porous*

Suggested activity

- Divide the pupils into groups and appoint a scribe to each. Ask them to brainstorm, and then record through brief notes, initial ideas for making a sweating machine. Its function is to explain to pupils in Year 3 how the human body sweats. *How will it be powered? Where the water will be stored? Why will it evaporate?* Hold a plenary session at which a spokesperson from each group can offer their ideas. (Ideas might include: a thin metal tray of water suspended over a row of light bulbs. To represent an increase in physical activity, more and more bulbs are lit. A piece of clingfilm suspended a few centimetres above the tray would catch the droplets as the water evaporated.)

Literacy

Page 18	Page 19
written explanation	visual explanation

Starting with the explanation of how the pot cooler works, ask the pupils to design a set of instructions for young elephants wishing to keep themselves cool. (Guidelines for instructions are on p 26 of these notes.)

Pages 20–21

Science

Key concepts

- Liquids other than water evaporate.
- Evaporation of some liquids can create hazards.

Key vocabulary

- *humidity, drought, fumes, spills, pollution, flammable, solvents*

Suggested activities

- Ask the pupils to list as many hazardous liquids they can think of that are used either in school or at home.
- How are these packaged so that the dangers they present are made clear to potential users?

Literacy

Page 20	Page 21
visual report	visual report

These pages are used as a featured example to teach pupils how to read and write **report** text. See pp 30–35 of these notes.

Challenge the pupils to extract from this visual report the necessary information to make notes for a written report on: *Evaporation: its uses and its dangers*. Encourage them to start by sorting all the information on the page into two categories – dangerous and useful – then to compose their opening paragraph.

Ask the pupils to find, in newspapers, in information books, or on the Internet, recounts of incidents where fires or explosions have been caused by evaporating liquids changing state to become hazardous gases.

Design a notice for a petrol station that warns simply and clearly that it is dangerous to bring naked flames to an area where petrol vapour is present.

© OUP: This page may be reproduced for use solely within the purchaser's school or college

Pages 22–23

Science

Key concepts
- Liquids other than water evaporate.
- Evaporation of some liquids can create hazards.

Key vocabulary
- *volatile, toxic, flammable, explosive, regulations, approved containers, ventilation, confined spaces*

Suggested activities
- The information on these pages develops the themes explored on pp 20–21. Ask the pupils to choose one of the products mentioned on both spreads and to design a single-sheet safety leaflet to accompany it. They should make sure they use a combination of clear and vivid illustrations, technical vocabulary where necessary, and straightforward instructions for safe use so that there can be no doubt in the user's mind about how this product can be used safely.
- The illustrations of visual icons to aid the identification of hazardous materials could be added to complement the work done on the previous spread.

Literacy

Page 22	Page 23
written explanation	written explanation

These pages add more detail to what has been expressed largely as a visual report on the previous spread. Encourage the pupils to analyse what extra information has been added here by the use of written and visual material, so that they can identify what they already knew and what they are now finding out.

Pages 24–25

Science

Key concepts
- Condensation is when a gas turns to a liquid.
- Condensation is the opposite of evaporation.
- Water vapour in the air may condense when it hits a cold surface.

Key vocabulary
- *condensation, water vapour, atmosphere*

Suggested activities
- Using a kettle, demonstrate how steam hitting a cold surface (tile or window pane) leaves drops of water behind. Ask the pupils where else they frequently see condensation, e.g. in the bathroom, on car windows.
- Produce a drinks can from a freezer. Ask, *where do the droplets of water come from?*

Literacy

Page 24	Page 25
written explanation	visual explanation

Using the sentence beginning '*The atmosphere holds…*', point out how commas are used within a list.

Using the sentence beginning '*This explains why…*', point out how a pair of commas can be used to make a complex sentence easier to understand by isolating an extra, yet vital, piece of information.

As a shared writing exercise ask the pupils to use the latter skill to rewrite sentences from the paragraph on dewponds (e.g. '*Farmers, in medieval times, dug saucer-shaped ponds*'; '*The ponds, which they first lined with straw, were then covered with clay and pebbles*').

© OUP: This page may be reproduced for use solely within the purchaser's school or college

Pages 26-27

Science

Key concept
- Scientific facts relate to everyday events.

Key vocabulary
- *condensation, extractor fans, ventilation*

Suggested activities
- Ask the pupils to be building inspectors in their own classroom. Can they find any areas where condensation is proving a problem, or where it could be a problem?
- As well as damp patches, can they think of any other hazards posed by large amounts of condensation, e.g. pools of water gathering near electrical sockets, condensation making surfaces slippery.

Literacy

Page 26	Page 27
*≶ *≶ *≶ written persuasion	*≶ *≶ *≶ written persuasion

These pages are used as featured examples to teach pupils how to read and write **persuasive** writing. See pp 42–47 of these notes.

As a shared writing exercise help the pupils compose the letter that Mr Swan sends back to Mr Adams *after* he has followed his suggestions.

Pages 28-29

Science

Key concepts
- Scientific evidence can be obtained by making careful observations.
- Conclusions should be drawn using terms of scientific knowledge and understanding.
- The boiling point of pure water is 100 °C.
- Prediction is an important part of scientific experimentation.

Key vocabulary
- *apparatus, probe, interface, data-logging software, graph*

Suggested activities
- Create a graph of a container of water being heated, which shows the temperature rising by 5 °C every minute, from 20 °C to 45 °C. Ask the pupils to predict what the next five readings will be.
- Using the evidence contained in *Observations and conclusions* on p 29, ask the pupils to list the reasons given why the water didn't behave as the graph would have predicted it would. (A further reason could be that the thermometer was not immersed to the correct depth.)

Literacy

Page 28	Page 29
⊢⊢⊢→ written recount	⊢⊢⊢→ visual recount

Discuss with the pupils why it is important that scientists write up their results after an experiment.

Ask the pupils to choose one of the sections from the foot of p 29 and, using the relevant notes from these two pages, write that section as part of the scientists' report.

Pages 30–31

Science

Key concepts
- Ideas can be turned into an investigation.
- Planning an investigation may help the pupils focus on relevant predictions.

Key vocabulary
- *investigation*

Suggested activities
- Ask the pupils to relate the plan outlined on these pages to the results expressed on the previous spread in order to make realistic predictions as to the outcome of the experiment.
- Hold a brainstorming session to generate ideas as to how the pupils' knowledge of ICT could be utilized to assist with the production of their plan. Apart from using word processing for the writing, do they have any specialist knowledge they could use as part of the recording process – would a database or a spreadsheet be relevant here? Have they ever used a 'computer data logger'? Could they use the Internet to discover more about it, or could they email senior schools in the area to find out more?

Literacy

Page 30	Page 31
written explanation	visual instructions

P 31 offers suggestions to the reader as to how they might go about planning their investigation. Ask the pupils to rewrite these in a more forceful way as a piece of instructional text that follows the guidelines set out on p 26 of these notes. (You may wish to divide the pupils into groups and give each group specific parts of the page to work on.)

Pages 32–33

Science

Key concepts
- Melting and boiling points can indicate the state of a substance at everyday temperatures.
- Changing the states of certain materials (e.g. liquifying gases) can provide valuable resources for medicine and technology.

Key vocabulary
- *melting point, boiling point, liquefied gas*

Suggested activities
- Ask, *if they were experimenting with the melting and boiling points of water, iron, and tungsten, what safety measures would they have to use and what special equipment do they think they might need?*
- Discuss extreme temperatures with the pupils. *How do active volcanoes threaten human environments? What do they know about lava? What happens when it cools? How was Pompeii preserved by the eruption of Mt. Etna? Can any creatures live in the extreme temperatures of the Arctic and Antarctic? How have they adapted for survival in such hostile conditions?*

Literacy

Page 32	Page 33
written report	visual report

Some of the facts represented in the table at the foot of p 33 can be found in the written report on the spread. Use this as an example of how note taking is a useful tool for extrapolating pieces of key information from continuous prose.

Ask the pupils to use this spread to make notes on the topic, 'Uses of liquefied gas'.

Pages 34–35

Science

Key concept
- Living things need oxygen and warmth to survive.

Key vocabulary
- *oxygen, water, freezing temperatures*

Suggested activities
- Ask the pupils to list more common-place, life-threatening incidents that are also a result of a lack of essential elements (e.g. drowning, smoke inhalation, choking, hypothermia). Ask them to produce scientific solutions to overcoming these dangers.
- Apollo 13 was saved by the clear-headed thinking of the scientists on Earth. Research other near disasters with the pupils where specialist knowledge combined with a lack of panic enabled people to survive, e.g. Ernest Shackleton's escape from the Antarctic, Captain Bligh's boat journey after the mutiny on the *Bounty*, Gladys Aylward's march with the children out of China, and Florence Nightingale's organization of the hospital at Scutari during the Crimean War.

Literacy

Page 34	Page 35
written recount	visual recount

These pages are used as a featured example to teach pupils how to read and write **recount** text. See pp 18–23 of these notes.

Discuss with the pupils which version is more exciting to read: the continuous text on p 34, or the abbreviated text and bullet point versions on p 35?

Which version recounts the information more efficiently? Widen the discussion to explore how different styles can impart the same information but for different purposes.

Pages 36–37

Science

Key concept
- Understanding scientific facts can save lives.

Key vocabulary
- *Space Shuttle, rubber seals, booster rocket*

Suggested activities
- Ask the pupils to use the spread as their primary source of reference to make scientific notes that chart the steps that led to the explosion in the Shuttle.
- Ask the pupils to use the Internet to try and find pictures of Earth taken from space, giving the same sort of view the astronauts in a Shuttle might have.

Literacy

Page 36	Page 37
visual recount	visual recount

These pages are used as a featured example to teach pupils how to read and write **recount** text. See pp 18–23 of these notes.

Ask the pupils to present as a playscript the conversation that took place between the engineers and the managers on 27 January. Make sure they include:

- engineers' reasons for not wanting the launch to go ahead;
- managers' reasons for wanting the launch to take place (e.g. the TV companies wanted exciting pictures, not another delay; scientific institutes had paid a lot of money for their experiments to be taken into space, and were angry about the delay);
- conversation that takes place *after* the disaster.

Pages 38–39

Science

Key concept
- Melting, freezing, condensing and evaporating are all changing states that can be reversed.

Key vocabulary
- *reversible, liquid crystals, permanent*

Suggested activities
- After revising the nature of the changing states undergone by chocolate sauce and ice-cream, ask the pupils to trace the changing states undergone by:
  - water being frozen as an ice cube, left in the sun and then frozen again;
  - squares of chocolate being melted, poured into moulds, and, after cooling, being sold as chocolate animals.
- Explore further the pupils' understanding of reversible and permanent changing states by challenging them to classify the contents of their lunches. *Is any food stuff truly reversible? Toast and baked potatoes cannot be reversed. Can a fruit salad? baked beans? Once frozen peas have been cooked is it possible to return them to their original state? What about dried fruit?*

Literacy

Page 38	Page 39
written report	visual and written reports

As a shared writing task ask the pupils to plan a non-chronological written report that investigates the different states witnessed by:

- a cook making scrambled egg on toast;
- a bricklayer building a wall.

Pages 40–41

Science

Key concept
- The changing states of wax (from solid to liquid to gas) allow a candle to burn.

Key vocabulary
- *vapour, molten, mould, granules*

Suggested activities
- Ask the pupils to create a flow chart that shows concisely how the changing states of candle wax, centred around a wick, create a constant flame.
- Extend the pupils' understanding of how the natures of different materials – in this case tallow and wax – affect technological developments. Dry reeds were often rolled in tallow to create thin rushlights that required holders such as those depicted in the photograph at the top of p 40. Explore with the pupils how the properties of beeswax allow for fatter candles, and also candlesticks, while the properties of tallow produce a thin light that needs a more delicate holder.

Literacy

Page 40	Page 41
written recount and explanation	visual instructions

Ask the pupils to create a safety manual to accompany the candle that they might make following the instructions on p 41.

© OUP: This page may be reproduced for use solely within the purchaser's school or college

Pages 42–43

Science

Key concepts
- When water evaporates from oceans, seas and lakes it condenses as clouds then falls as rain that collects in streams and rivers and returns to oceans, seas, and lakes.
- Evaporation and condensation are reversible processes.

Key vocabulary
- *substance, water vapour, evaporates, condenses, cycle*

Suggested activity
- Once the children have understood the nature of the water cycle ask them to predict what the effects would be at stages 3, 4 and 5 if the water cycle was interrupted (e.g. plant and animal life that depended on the mountain stream would die out; as the rivers became stagnant pools, fish would die from lack of oxygen; supplies of drinking water and hydro-electric power would dry up).

Literacy

Page 42	Page 43
⊙→⊙⊙	⊙⊙
written explanation	visual explanation

Read the written explanation on pp 42–43 of the pupils' book with the pupils. Discuss its language features. Present its content as a visual skeleton. Look at the accompanying visual explanation on pp 42–43 of the pupils' book. Discuss with the children whether they think the artwork assists or hinders their understanding of the written explanation.

Ask the pupils to tell the story of the raindrop featured in the visual explanation as an imaginative piece of fiction that remains rooted in fact. Encourage them to use the five senses throughout their story, especially when they are describing the different states the raindrop encounters. You might like to precede the story with a brainstorming session.

Pages 44–45

Science

Key concept
- Global warming causes changing states that may, in turn, cause flooding, droughts, and crop failures.

Key vocabulary
- *global warming, greenhouse gases, communities, energy consumption, alternative energy, solar panels, wind generators*

Suggested activities
- Ask the pupils to analyse the arguments presented on this page from a scientific point of view. Ask questions such as: *How will changing states cause flooding? If the rise in temperature releases more water as liquid, will this create more rain? What will cause the droughts?*
- Debate the question: 'It is our fault there are droughts and floods; it is not the fault of the weather.'

Literacy

Page 44	Page 45
*≶ *≶ *≶	*≶ *≶ *≶
written persuasion	written persuasion

These pages are used as featured examples to teach pupils how to read and write **persuasive** writing. See pp 42–47 of these notes.

As a shared writing exercise, work with the pupils to produce a piece of written persuasion that might be written by pupils living in a community in the foothills of the Himalayas. They have no light in their school, no heat in their houses, no readily available source of fuel, and no method of transport except walking. They are trying to persuade their audience that they should be allowed these things.

Page 46

Science

Key concept
- To use vocabulary associated with changing states.

Suggested activity
- Use these pages to search for the meanings of key vocabulary to further the pupils' understanding of different aspects of changing states. Identify words from reading that are unknown and use the **glossary** to further understanding and to clarify information learnt.

Literacy

Use these pages to demonstrate how to locate information confidently and efficiently using a glossary.

- Remind pupils of the purpose of a glossary – to explain the meaning of words that are specific to the subject of the text.
- Using some of the key words identified in both the text and these teacher's notes, show how to scan the glossary to find some of the meanings. Point out that the technical words are in alphabetical order rather than subject order.

Page 47-48

Science

Key concepts
- Scientific evidence is found from a number of different sources.
- Use **index** to locate information in different parts of the book

Literacy

Use this page to teach the pupils the purpose and function of a **bibliography**.

Point out to pupils that a bibliography:

- collates all the references to other sources made in the text;
- provides a reference point for further reading;
- avoids the author being challenged for using someone else's work (plagiarism);
- is organized either by date of publication or alphabetically using the surname of the author;
- provides the ISBN number (International Standard Book Number) as well as the title of the reference;
- contains some of the following sources: books, websites, articles, periodicals and journals.

Use the bibliography to find further details about one area of changing states. Ensure the pupils use a wide range of sources referenced.

Discuss how different source material is organized. Compare details provided in *Changing State* with material found in a different source.

Use the index to find specific information. Point out the following:

- At times, it is quicker to use an index rather than the contents.
- An index sometimes doesn't take you to the information you want – you may have to go to a number of pages.
- *Skimming* is a more general approach than *scanning*. Both skills can be used to obtain information quickly but have different purposes, for example, scanning when you want to know something specific and skimming if you want a general overview before obtaining details or making a close read.

Teaching pupils how to read and write recount text

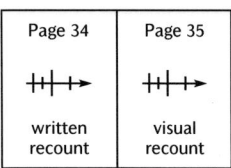

Reading a recount text

Read pp 34–35 of *Changing State* pupils' book with the pupils. You will also need:

- the written recount on pp 34–35 (the text-only version on p 21 of this book can be enlarged/photocopied/made into an OHT for annotation);
- p 20 of these notes enlarged/photocopied/made into an OHT for annotation.

SHARED READING ACTIVITY

Audience and purpose

Talk about how the intended audience and purpose affect the language and layout.

Audience – pupils in Year 5, who may be familiar with the story from the filmed version.

Purpose – to explain, from a non-fiction, non-emotive, scientific point of view, how the changing states of various materials played crucial roles in the drama.

SHARED WRITING ACTIVITY

Content and organization

Demonstrate to the pupils how the content of this recount text is organized by showing it as a recount skeleton. (See p 23 of these notes.)

SHARED READING ACTIVITY

Language features and style

Return to the text and talk about the way language features have been used to achieve the effects the author intended. (See annotated example on p 22 of these notes). If some of the pupils are familiar with the film version, you could discuss how suitable/unsuitable these language features would be if the author was retelling the story as a piece of dramatic prose.

Key language features for a non-fiction version are:

- written in the past tense;
- focus on specifics – people, places, dates;
- words to show time order, e.g. *On 21 July ... By the time... Months later.*

INDEPENDENT ACTIVITY

Use the exciting, human, aspects of the story of Apollo 13 to inspire the pupils to create an oral version that they tell to the rest of the class. They should aim to use their own words as much as possible.

Encourage them to practise the key skill of making their own notes from the text on pp 34–35 of the pupils' book. They will need to be selective. They should avoid copying the scientific style of the book, adapting the facts for a more expressive story of human interest. Make sure any quotes they use are relevant to the tale they are telling.

Impress on them that the best storytellers don't read out what they have written, but use their notes as stepping stones to guide them through the tale.

© OUP: This page may be reproduced for use solely within the purchaser's school or college

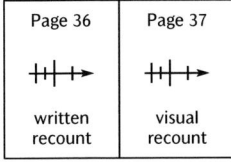

written recount | visual recount

Writing a recount text

Use pp 36–37 of *Changing State* pupils' book as a basis for the pupils' own recount texts.

You will need:

- the visual recount on pp 36–37;
- p 20 of these notes enlarged/photocopied/made into an OHT for annotation.

Content and organization

Revise the content and organization of the recount text from the previous session (see p 23 of these notes).

Ask pairs of children to discuss the visual recount on pp 36–37 of the pupils' book and identify and extract the key events to create a recount skeleton.

PAIRED READING AND WRITING ACTIVITY

Language features and style

Remind pupils of the language features and style of recount texts (see p 20 of these notes).

Audience and purpose

Discuss the audience for the pupils' recounts (other class members) and the purpose (to retell an actual historical event).

SHARED READING ACTIVITY

Demonstrate, by writing an introductory paragraph, how to set the scene. Remind the pupils that their recount should be written in the third person (this is not a first-person account from someone who was there). Although it is a moving story their writing will be a formal and impersonal recount, e.g.

The launch of the Space Shuttle Challenger on 28th January 1986 was one of the greatest disasters of the American space programme. Less than two minutes after lift-off the Shuttle exploded. All seven astronauts were killed.

Ask the pupils to work in pairs to create oral suggestions for the first sentence of the next paragraph, e.g.
The original date for the launch had been 22nd January.

Ask the pupils to suggest how further information – particularly dates and words that clearly show the order of events – can be included, e.g.
Finally, on 27th January, after four days of delays, it was decided that the Challenger would be launched the next day. During that night the temperature dropped to −8° Centigrade. It was so cold the rubber seals in the booster rockets froze.

INDEPENDENT WRITING ACTIVITY

Ask the pupils to continue the written recount.

About recount text

Audience and purpose

Audience – someone who may not know much about the events.

Purpose – to retell events that actually happened.

> Sometimes you may know more about the age or interests of your reader

Content and organization

- **introductory paragraph** sets the scene, so the reader has all the basic facts needed to understand the recount
- **introduction** often also hints at the main event of the recount
- events written in **chronological order** – time order
- **closing statement** – sentence(s) or paragraph to bring the recount to an end

> Answer the questions who? what? when? where?

> Use your introductory sentence to help you write your conclusion. If the introduction is a question then answer it in your conclusion

> First this happened... then this happened... next...

Language features

- written in the **past tense** because these are specific events that only happened once
- focus on **specific people, places, dates** etc.
- may be written in the **first** or **third person**
- **words and devices** to show **time order**

> This usually means proper nouns, so remember the capital letters!

> Stick to one or the other – don't mix them up

> First..., next..., finally..., In 1950..., Some weeks later...

The basic skeleton for making notes is a timeline

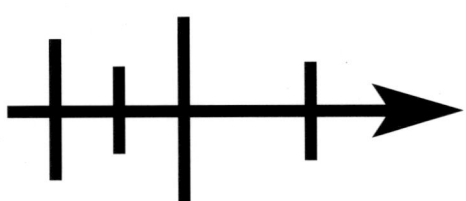

An example of a recount text

By the time Apollo 13 was launched on 11 April 1970 the public were beginning to take the success of Moon missions for granted. But, at 9:08 pm on 13 April, some 200,000 miles from Earth, the crew felt a sharp bang followed by a series of vibrations. Lunar module pilot Jack Swigert saw a warning light flash on and calmly reported over the radio link to Earth, "Houston, we've had a problem here".

Looking out of the window of the command module Jim Lovell saw debris and gas evaporating into space. The instruments showed that one of the main oxygen tanks was empty and the second was losing pressure rapidly. An explosion had destroyed one tank and badly damaged the other.

The situation was critical – but not yet fatal. The Moon landing was immediately abandoned as the astronauts and ground crew worked frantically to devise a plan to return the crippled craft to Earth. The craft had not been designed with enough power to reverse direction in mid-flight, so it had to continue on its outward journey, swinging around the Moon before heading back to Earth. In the meantime the crew moved into the lunar-landing module to use the oxygen, water and power supplies that it carried.

The crew spent the following days in freezing temperatures with just a cupful of water to drink each day as they conserved their remaining power and water supplies. But the plan went well. A few hours before landing they returned to the dark command module, switched on its electric circuits, and prayed that there would be enough power left for a safe touchdown. With baited breath the ground crew waited. Then, at 12:07 pm on 17 April, nearly four days after the explosion that threatened to maroon them in space, cheering erupted as the crew of Apollo 13 parachuted safely into the Pacific Ocean.

Language features and style of recount text

Introductory paragraph — By the time Apollo 13 was launched on 11 April 1970 the public were beginning to take the success of Moon missions for granted. But, at 9:08 pm on 13 April, some 200,000 miles from Earth, the crew felt a sharp bang followed by a series of vibrations. *Specific people/places/dates*

Introduction hints at the main events of the recount — Lunar module pilot Jack Swigert saw a warning light flash on and calmly reported over the radio link to Earth, "Houston, we've had a problem here".

Looking out of the window of the command module Jim Lovell saw debris and gas evaporating into space. The instruments showed that one of the main oxygen tanks was empty and the second was losing pressure rapidly. An explosion had destroyed one tank and badly damaged the other. *Past tense throughout*

Third person throughout — The situation was critical – but not yet fatal. The Moon landing was immediately abandoned as the astronauts and ground crew worked frantically to devise a plan to return the crippled craft to Earth. The craft had not been designed with enough power to reverse direction in mid-flight, so it had to continue on its outward journey, swinging around the Moon before heading back to Earth. In the meantime the crew moved into the lunar-landing module to use the oxygen, water and power supplies that it carried.

Time order devices — The crew spent the following days in freezing temperatures with just a cupful of water to drink each day as they conserved their remaining power and water supplies. But the plan went well. A few hours before landing they returned to the dark command module, switched on its electric circuits, and prayed that there would be enough power left for a safe touchdown. With baited breath the ground crew waited. Then, at 12:07 pm on 17 April, nearly four days after the explosion that threatened to maroon them in space, cheering erupted as the crew of Apollo 13 parachuted safely into the Pacific Ocean. *Closing statement*

© OUP: This page may be reproduced for use solely within the purchaser's school or college

If you are using this text with other year groups then also highlight these features:

Y3/P4
- Noticing and investigating a range of other devices for presenting texts (**e.g. captions and headings, inset text**).

Y4/P5
- Using commas to mark grammatical boundaries within sentences.

Y6/P7
- Revising work on complex sentences (**identifying main clauses, ways of connecting clauses, constructing complex sentences, appropriate use of punctuation**).

Content and organization of the recount text

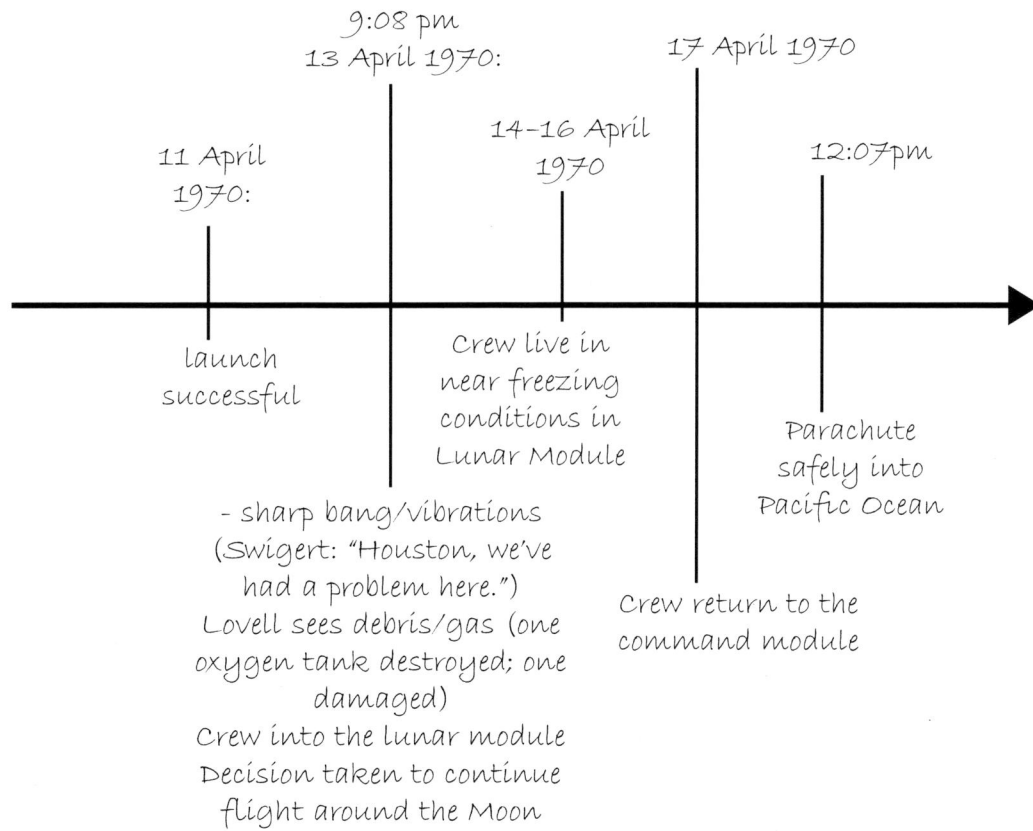

Teaching pupils how to read and write instruction text

Page 12
written instructions

Reading an instruction text

Read p 12 of *Changing State* pupils' book with the pupils. You will need:

- the written instruction on p 12 (the text-only version on p 27 of these notes can be enlarged/photocopied/made into an OHT for annotation);
- p 26 of these notes enlarged/photocopied/made into an OHT for annotation.

SHARED READING ACTIVITY

Audience and purpose

Talk about how the intended audience and purpose affects the language and layout.

Audience – pupils and interested adults who wish to know how to make an air thermometer.

Purpose – to make a thermometer that works efficiently and demonstrates the basic principles of measuring temperature.

SHARED WRITING ACTIVITY

Content and organization

Demonstrate to the pupils how the content of this instruction text is organized by showing it as a visual instruction skeleton (see page 29 of these notes).

SHARED READING ACTIVITY

Language features and style

Return to the text and talk about the way the language features have been used to achieve the effects the author intended (see annotated example on p 28 of these notes).

Note important features for use in the pupils' own writing:

- use of the imperative – *push, turn, pull*;
- numbered sequencing;
- necessary detail – *turn the bottle upside down*;
- factual descriptive words – *coloured water, card strip*.

INDEPENDENT ACTIVITY

Set the pupils the challenge of preparing an instructional talk designed to be given on TV. (You may like to introduce this topic by showing the class brief clips of TV presenters explaining how to make something, how to cook, how to paint etc.)

Use the visual instruction skeleton to prepare a talk for a children's science programme about making a thermometer.

Impress on them the importance of reducing their knowledge from a mass of material, through notes, down to a few headings on a single sheet of paper. They can use the headings as prompts to carry them through their speech.

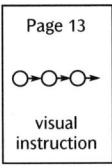

Page 13
visual instruction

Writing an instruction text

Use p 13 of *Changing State* pupils' book as the basis for the pupils' own explanation texts. You will need:

- the visual instruction on p 13;
- p 26 of these notes enlarged/photocopied/made into an OHT for annotation.

Content and organization

SHARED READING ACTIVITY

Revise the content and organization of the instruction text from the previous session (see page 29 of these notes). Remind the pupils that, with instruction texts, it is vital that no steps are left out and that all necessary detail must be included.

INDEPENDENT/ PAIRED READING AND WRITING ACTIVITY

Ask pairs of pupils to discuss the visual instructions on p 13 of the pupils' book and make instruction skeleton notes (see example below) using as much detailed information as they can gather from the page.

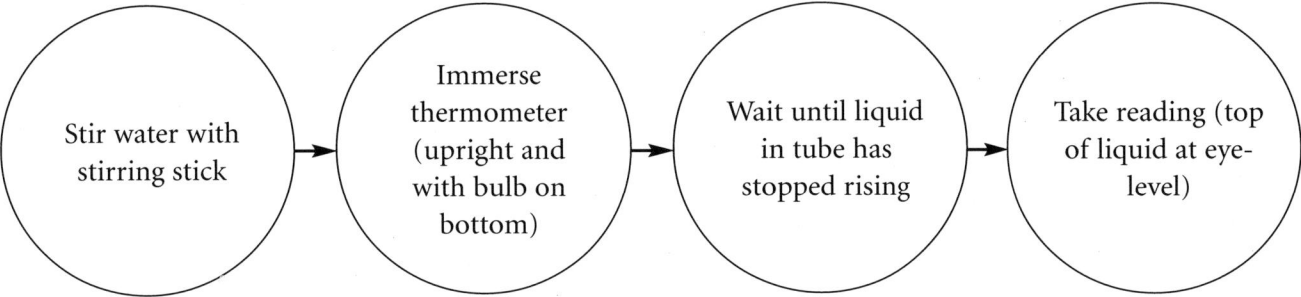

Language features and style

Remind pupils of the language features and style of instruction text (see p 26 of these notes).

SHARED WRITING ACTIVITY

Audience and purpose

Discuss the audience for the pupils' instructions (e.g. other pupils who are not familiar with using digital thermometers) and the purpose (to give clear instructions in their use in the classroom experiment).

Demonstrate how to write the first instruction by scribing it for them, e.g.
Gather the necessary equipment: a beaker filled with water, a stirring stick, a digital thermometer.

Remind the pupils that you are using the imperative.

Ask the pupils to make suggestions for the next instruction. Remind them they must not miss out any necessary detail.

INDEPENDENT WRITING ACTIVITY

Using their experiences in the shared writing, encourage the children to complete the set of instructions for the children in the year below them to follow.

© OUP: This page may be reproduced for use solely within the purchaser's school or college

About instruction text

Audience and purpose

Audience – someone who needs to use the instructions.

Purpose – to tell someone how to do or make something.

> Sometimes you may know more about the age or interests of your reader

Content and organization

- **title** (or opening sentence) tells what is to be done or made
- **list** of what is needed
- sometimes **picture(s) or diagram(s)**
- the instructions are written as a sequence in **time order**

> How to make a ...

> You will need: 2 sheets of A4 white paper, coloured pens ... etc

> 1. Draw a person ...
> 2. Cut it out ...

Language features

- written in the **imperative,** as if the writer is talking directly to the reader telling him or her what to do
- numbers or words and devices to show the **sequence** of the steps
- all **necessary detail** included (for instance, *how many, how far, how long*)
- **factual descriptive words,** not like the descriptions in a story

> Draw a person ... Cut it out ...

> First ... Next ... Finally ...

> 2 A4 sheets of white paper

> NOT two lovely sheets of clean, crisp, white paper!

The basic skeleton for making notes is a flowchart

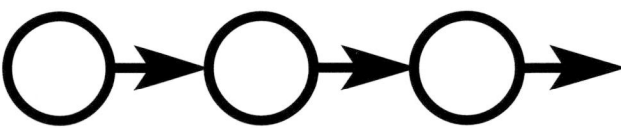

An example of an instruction text

How to make an air thermometer

You will need:

Narrow plastic tube
Plasticene
Strip of card, marked with a scale
500 ml plastic lemonade bottle
Coloured water in a plastic beaker

1. Push one end of the plastic tube 2 or 3 cm down inside the neck of the plastic lemonade bottle.
2. Firmly push Plasticene around the tube at the neck of the bottle to seal the tube in position.
3. Turn the bottle upside down. Squeeze the bottle gently, then dip the free end of the tube in the coloured water.
4. Partly release the bottle to draw a drop of coloured water up into the tube.
5. Pull the tube from the water, then release the water so that the drop moves to the middle of the tube (you may need to try this procedure several times before you get the drop in the right position).
6. Turn the bottle and tube back upright.
7. Draw a scale on a card strip and tape the card strip to the tube.
8. Hold your thermometer in warm water. Mark the position of the coloured water drop on the card.
9. Hold your thermometer in iced water and again mark the position of the coloured water drop. Observe how the drop has moved.

Language features and style of the instruction text

Title – what is to be done

How to make an air thermometer

List of essentials

You will need:

Narrow plastic tube
Plasticene
Strip of card, marked with a scale
500 ml plastic lemonade bottle
Coloured water in a plastic beaker

Instructions in exact sequence

Imperatives

Numbered steps

1. Push one end of the plastic tube 2 or 3 cm down inside the neck of the plastic lemonade bottle.
2. Firmly push Plasticene around the tube at the neck of the bottle to seal the tube in position.
3. Turn the bottle upside down. Squeeze the bottle gently, then dip the free end of the tube in the coloured water. — *Necessary detail*
4. Partly release the bottle to draw a drop of coloured water up into the tube. — *Factual description*
5. Pull the tube from the water, then release the water so that the drop moves to the middle of the tube (you may need to try this procedure several times before you get the drop in the right position).
6. Turn the bottle and tube back upright.
7. Draw a scale on a card strip and tape the card strip to the tube.
8. Hold your thermometer in warm water. Mark the position of the coloured water drop on the card.
9. Hold your thermometer in iced water and again mark the position of the coloured water drop. Observe how the drop has moved.

If you are using this text with other year groups then also highlight these features:

Y3/P4 ◆ Read and following simple instructions.
Y4/P5 ◆ Writing clear instructions using conventions learned from reading.
Y6/P7 ◆ Revising the language features and grammatical features of instructional texts.

Content and organization of the instruction text

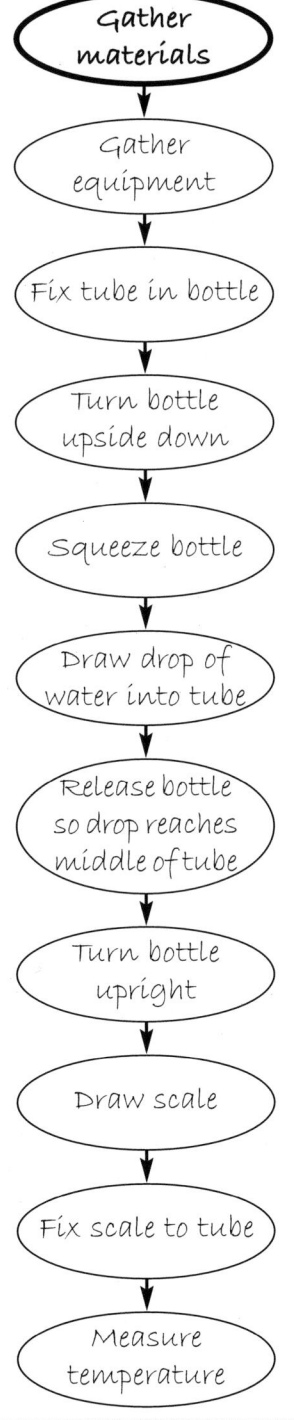

© OUP: This page may be reproduced for use solely within the purchaser's school or college

Teaching pupils how to read and write report text

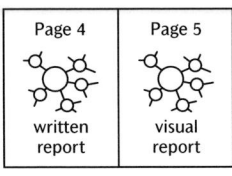

Reading a report text

Read p 4 of *Changing State* pupils' book with the pupils. You will need:

- the written report on p 4 (the text-only version on p 33 of these notes can be enlarged/photocopied/made into an OHT for annotation);
- p 32 of these notes enlarged/photocopied/made into an OHT for annotation.

SHARED READING ACTIVITY

Audience and purpose

Talk about how the intended audience and purpose affects language and layout.

Audience – pupils who may or may not know about the nature of materials.

Purpose – to summarize key facts about materials and to define their different properties.

SHARED WRITING ACTIVITY

Content and organization

Demonstrate to the pupils how the content of this report text has been organized by showing its contents as a report skeleton (see p 35 of these notes).

SHARED READING ACTIVITY

Language features and style

Return to the text and talk about the way language has been used to achieve the effects the author intended (see annotated example of the text on p 34 of these notes). The same methods can be used by the pupils in their own writing.

Explore with the pupils this concept:

INDEPENDENT ACTIVITY

- note making should fillet passages for relevant information and present ideas that are effectively grouped and linked.

The pupils' goal is to make notes that will be the basis of a guessing game for the rest of the class.

Make a set of cards – one for each member of the class – that carry the names of solids, liquids and gases, e.g. brick, ice cube, milk, mercury, oxygen, carbon dioxide. When the pupils have been given their cards ask them to use the skeleton to generate three questions they can use to discover what type of material is on the other pupils' cards, e.g:

- *Can you pour it?*
- *Can it be compressed?*
- *Does it have a fixed shape?*

When they have decided on their questions ask them to use them to see if they can discover the nature of the material on each other's cards.

© OUP: This page may be reproduced for use solely within the purchaser's school or college

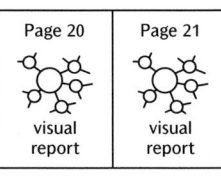

Writing a report text

Use pp 20–21 of *Changing State* pupils' book as a basis for the pupils' own report texts. You will need:

- the visual report on pp 20–21;
- page 32 of these notes enlarged/photocopied/made into an OHT for annotation.

SHARED READING ACTIVITY

Content and organization

Revise the content and organization of the report text from the previous session (see p 35 of these notes).

Ask pairs of pupils to read the visual report on pp 20–21 of the pupils' book and begin to discuss how the different sections can be used as the basis for a report skeleton on evaporation. The teacher acts as scribe and creates the report skeleton, adding and deleting according to the pupils' suggestions.

INDEPENDENT/PAIRED READING AND WRITING ACTIVITY

Language features and style

Remind pupils of the language features and style of reports (see p 32 of these notes). Remind them to keep their work impersonal.

SHARED WRITING ACTIVITY

Audience and purpose

Tell the children they are going to use the report skeleton as the starting point for writing a report about evaporation. Explain that it will be kept as a resource for children in their year group. It will be given to pupils who might have missed doing this topic in science because they were away from school. What does their target audience know already? Remind them that the job of their report is to pass on information.

Divide the class into groups and, still acting as scribe, experiment with writing clear opening statements, e.g.

Evaporation is important. It helps us keep cool. It allows things to dry. It makes the rain fall and flowers smell.

Challenge the writing groups to complete a whole paragraph about one of the specific areas that have been mentioned in the introduction – e.g. *cooling, odours, drying or the water cycle* – using information outlined in the report skeleton.

INDEPENDENT WRITING ACTIVITY

Ask the pupils to write a third paragraph independently.

About report text

Audience and purpose

Audience – someone who wants to know about the topic.

Purpose – to describe what something is like.

> Sometimes you may know more about the age or interests of your reader

Content and organization

- **non-chronological** information
- **introductory sentence or paragraph** says what the report is going to be about
- the information is sorted into groups or **categories**
- reports may include short pieces of explanation

> This means it ISN'T written in time order, like a story or recount

> What something looks like, where it is found...

Language features

- written in the **present tense**
- usually **general nouns and pronouns** (not particular people or things)
- **factual descriptive words**, not like the descriptions in a story
- words and devices that show **comparison and contrast**
- **third person** writing to make the report **impersonal and formal**
- **technical words and phrases** – which you may need to explain to the reader
- use of **examples** to help the reader understand the technical words

> You would write about dogs in general, not a particular dog

> You would say powerful beams, not beautiful bright beams

> Expressions like have in common, the same as..., on the other hand, however...

> Unusual words that go with the topic such as, canine, translucent and wing span

> Wingspan is the distance between the tips of a bird's outstretched wings

The basic skeleton for making notes is a spidergram

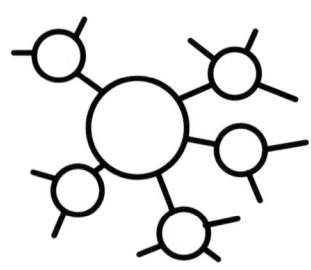

An example of a report text

Solid, liquid or gas?

Matter

Everything is made from matter. Matter is a general word for all the different materials and substances that make up the world. Rock, metal, plastic and glass are matter, and so are soil, water and air. Living things are matter, as are wood, leather and all materials that grew as parts of plants and animals.

Although there are thousands of different substances, matter usually takes one of just three forms: solid, liquid or gas. These forms of matter are called 'states'. Water flowing in a river is in the liquid state. The state of a stone or an iceberg is 'solid'. The air in the atmosphere is a gas.

Each state has its special properties. A solid has shape: it can be picked up and turned around. A liquid flows and changes shape: it takes the shape of the container into which it is poured. A gas can be squeezed into a smaller volume: this happens, for example, when a bicycle tyre is inflated with a pump.

Language features and style of the report text

Solid, liquid or gas?

Matter

[*Precise, introductory statement*]

Everything is made from matter. Matter is a general word for all the different materials and substances that make up the world. Rock, metal, plastic and glass are matter, and so are soil, water and air. Living things are matter, as are wood, leather and all materials that grew as parts of plants and animals.

[*Impersonal style throughout*]

[*Use of examples*]

Although there are thousands of different substances, matter usually takes one of just three forms: solid, liquid or gas. These forms of matter are called 'states'. Water flowing in a river is in the liquid state. The state of a stone or an iceberg is 'solid'. The air in the atmosphere is a gas.

[*Technical words*]

[*Not particular nouns – simply any/all rivers, icebergs etc.*]

Each state has its special properties. A solid has shape: it can be picked up and turned around. A liquid flows and changes shape: it takes the shape of the container into which it is poured. A gas can be squeezed into a smaller volume: this happens, for example, when a bicycle tyre is inflated with a pump.

[*Punctuation device for introducing examples – takes the place of phrases like: 'such as' or 'for example'*]

If you are using this text with other year groups then also highlight these features:

Y3/P4 ◆ Reading information passages, and identifying main points or gist of text.

Y4/P5 ◆ Identifying features of non-fiction texts in print (e.g. **headings, lists, bullet points, captions**).

Y6/P7 ◆ Securing understanding of the features of non-chronological reports.

Content and organization of the report text

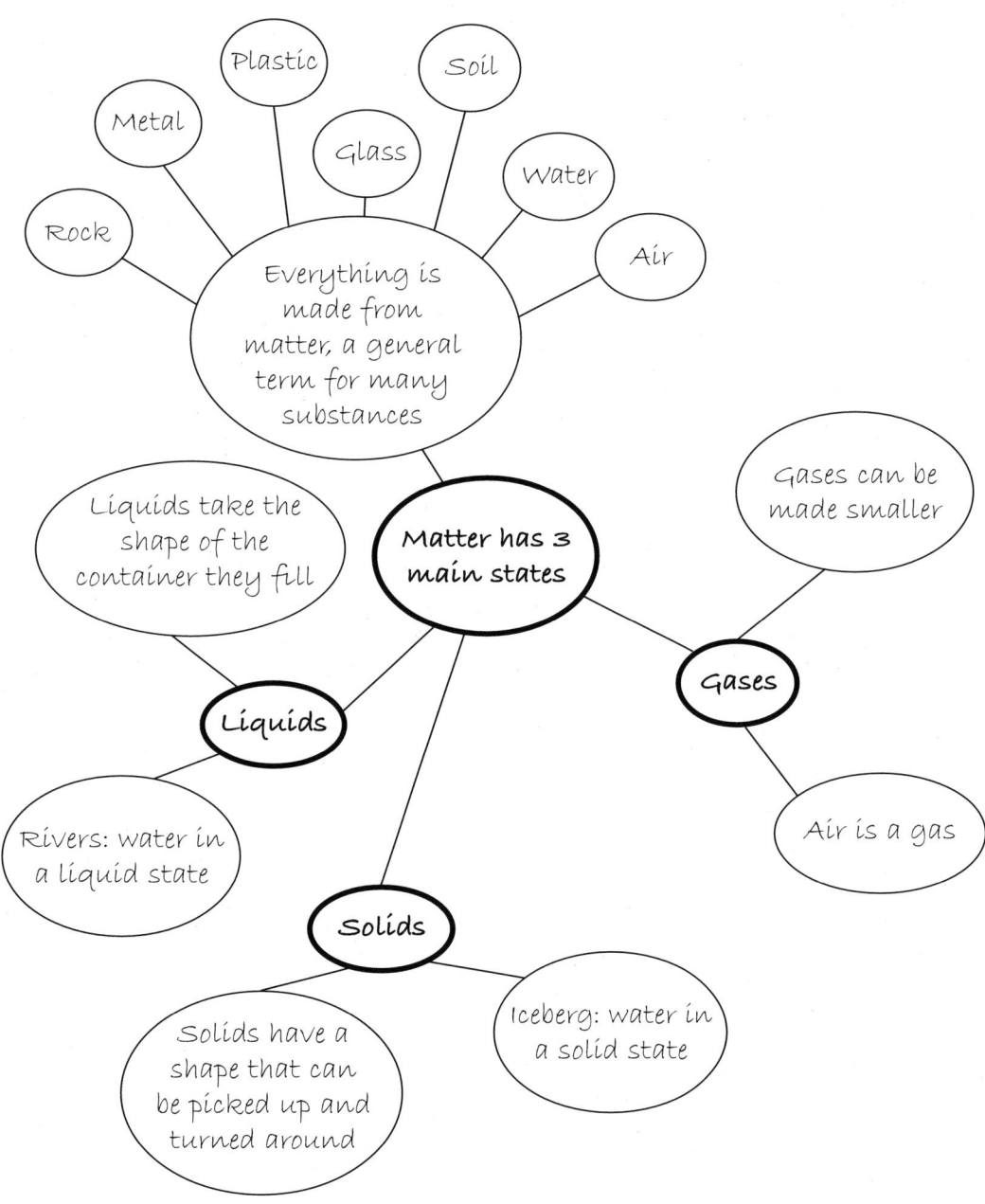

© OUP: This page may be reproduced for use solely within the purchaser's school or college

35

Teaching pupils how to read and write explanation text

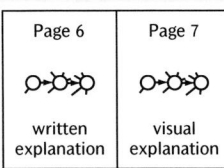

Reading an explanation text

Read pp 6–7 of *Changing State* pupils' book with the pupils. You will need:

- the written explanation on pp 6–7 (the text-only version on p 39 of these notes can be enlarged/photocopied/made into an OHT for annotation);
- p 38 of these notes enlarged/photocopied/made into an OHT for annotation.

SHARED READING ACTIVITY

Audience and purpose

Talk about how the intended audience and purpose affect the language and layout.

Audience – pupils in Year 5 with no previous specialist knowledge of the subject.

Purpose – to explain, as an initial example that can be applied to other types of matter, how water can be made to change its state by heating and cooling.

Content and organization

SHARED WRITING ACTIVITY

Demonstrate to the pupils how the content of this explanation text is organized by showing it as a visual cyclical flowchart. (See p 41 of these notes.) As the nature of water allows for its changes in state to be reversible, this particular text can be presented as a cycle. Other changing states, e.g. bread to toast or to breadcrumbs, are irreversible and would have to be presented as a multiple effect flowchart.

Language features and style

Return to the text and talk about the way language features have been used to achieve the effects the author intended. (See annotated example on p 40 of these notes).

SHARED READING ACTIVITY

Important features for the pupils' own writing include:

- present tense;
- third person;
- general, nor particular, nouns;
- factual, not imaginative, description;
- technical vocabulary;
- words that show sequence.

INDEPENDENT ACTIVITY

Explain to the pupils that the concepts on pp 6–7 of the pupils' book can be quite difficult for younger pupils to understand. Challenge them to make them more accessible by turning the explanations on the changes undergone by water when it freezes, melts, boils, and evaporates into a script that they can act out to the pupils in Year 4.

They could include the following – or similar – characters:

- Liquido;
- Cool Cube;
- HeatMan;
- The Steamy Seven and The Dancing Droplets.

© OUP: This page may be reproduced for use solely within the purchaser's school or college

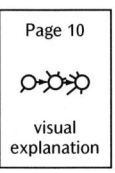

Page 10

visual explanation

Writing an explanation text

Use p 10 of *Changing State* pupils' book as a basis for the pupils' own explanation texts. You will need:

◆ the visual explanation on p 10;
◆ p 38 of these notes enlarged/photocopied/made into an OHT for annotation.

SHARED READING ACTIVITY

Content and organization

Revise the content and organization of the explanation text from the previous session (see p 41 of these notes).

INDEPENDENT/ PAIRED READING AND WRITING ACTIVITY

The pupils, working in pairs, should explore the visual explanation on p 10 and make explanation skeleton notes (see below). Notes should include details from the pictures and captions in addition to any information pupils already know. Act as a scribe during a discussion session in which the pupils suggest, assess and compare their different ideas. Ensure they have all understood the proper use of the technical vocabulary.

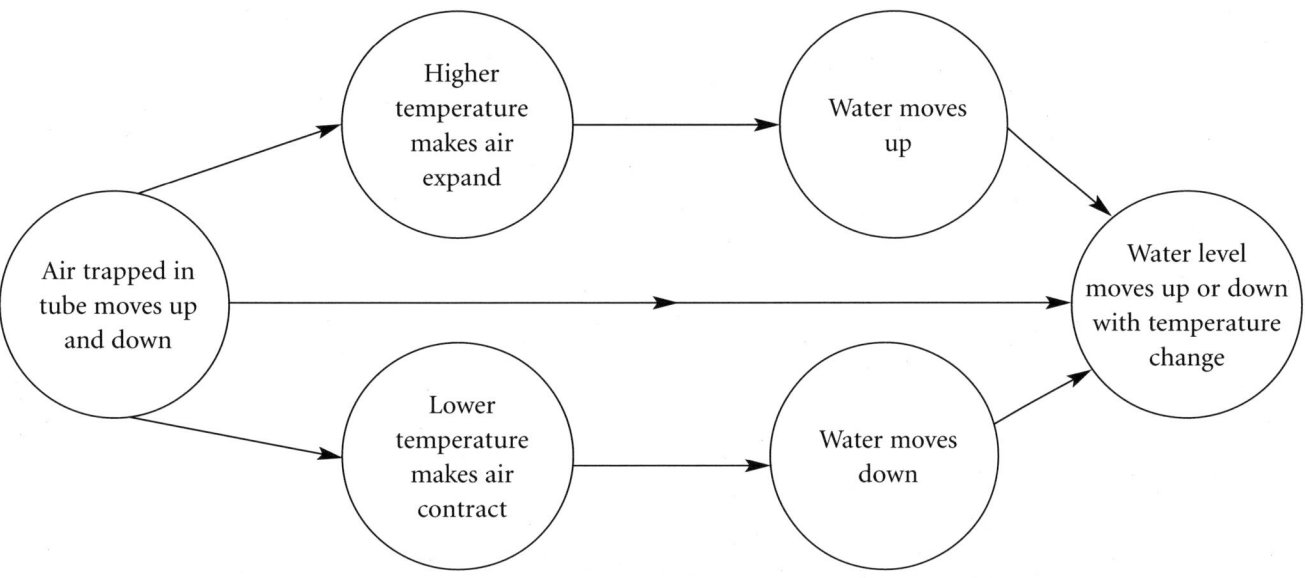

SHARED WRITING ACTIVITY

Language features and style

Before starting this activity remind the pupils of the language features and style of explanations (see p 38 of these notes).

Audience and purpose

Discuss with the pupils the possibility of turning their notes into an explanatory leaflet for a Year 4 class who know nothing at all about Galileo's invention.

Divide the class into groups and challenge them to devise:

◆ a *title* that will make clear to the Year 4 pupils what the leaflet is about;
◆ the opening *general statement* that introduces the subject;
◆ a *glossary* of the key technical terms;
◆ the *first paragraph* that explains, in logical steps, how Galileo's thermometer is constructed and how it will record the changes in temperature.

INDEPENDENT WRITING ACTIVITY

Ask the pupils to write the next paragraph independently, explaining how the trapped air is affected by the changing temperature.

© OUP: This page may be reproduced for use solely within the purchaser's school or college

About explanation text

Audience and purpose

Audience – someone who wants to understand the process (how or why it happens).

Purpose – to explain how or why something happens.

(Sometimes you may know more about the age or interests of your reader)

Content and organization

- **title** often asks a question, or says clearly what the explanation is about
- text often opens with **general statement(s)** to introduce important words or ideas
- the process is then written in a **series of logical steps**, usually in **time order**
- sometimes **picture(s) or diagram(s)**

(This happens... then this happens... next...)

Language features

- **third person** writing to make the explanation **impersonal and formal**
- written in the **present tense**
- usually **general nouns and pronouns** (not particular people or things)
- **factual descriptive words**, not like the descriptions in a story
- **technical words and phrases** – which you may need to explain to the reader
- words and devices that show **sequence**
- words and devices that show **cause and effect**

(You would say powerful beams, not beautiful bright beams)

(You would write about dogs in general, not a particular dog)

(Unusual words that go with the topic such as, canine, translucent and wing span)

(First..., next..., finally)

(If..., then... This happens because... This means that...)

The basic skeleton for making notes is a flowchart

(The explanation skeleton can change depending on the sort of process)

An example of an explanation text

Changing state

Water is a single substance, but it exists in three different states. At normal room temperature, around 20°C, water is liquid. Liquid water can be made to change its state by heating or cooling.

Changes of state have different names, depending on the start and finish states. Melting, for example, is the change of state from solid to liquid.

A liquid can change to a gas both by evaporation and by boiling. Water evaporates into the air at all temperatures. At room temperature this change is quite slow, but evaporation speeds up when the water is heated. Eventually the change becomes so fast that steam bubbles grow inside the liquid. The water is then boiling.

Language features and style of the explanation text

Changing state

Water is a single substance, but it exists in three different states. At normal room temperature, around 20°C, water is liquid. Liquid water can be made to change its state by heating or cooling.

Changes of state have different names, depending on the start and finish states. Melting, for example, is the change of state from solid to liquid.

A liquid can change to a gas both by evaporation and by boiling. Water evaporates into the air at all temperatures. At room temperature this change is quite slow, but evaporation speeds up when the water is heated. Eventually the change becomes so fast that steam bubbles grow inside the liquid. The water is then boiling.

Annotations:

- Use of the passive is an example of the formal style *(pointing to "can be made to")*
- Technical vocabulary used throughout the explanation *(pointing to "evaporation")*
- Words to show time order
- Present tense used throughout *(pointing to "exists")*
- Impersonal/formal writing throughout; no mention of 'you' or 'we'
- The sequence of logical steps is framed by the use of such terms as: 'At room temperature ... eventually ... then'.

If you are using this text with other year groups then also highlight these features:

Y3/P4 — ◆ Noting where commas occur in reading and discussing their functions.

Y4/P5 — ◆ Identifying from the examples the key features of explanatory texts: **purpose, structure, language features, presentation**.

Y6/P7 — ◆ Appraising a text quickly and effectively; retrieving information from it; finding information quickly.

Content and organization of the explanation text

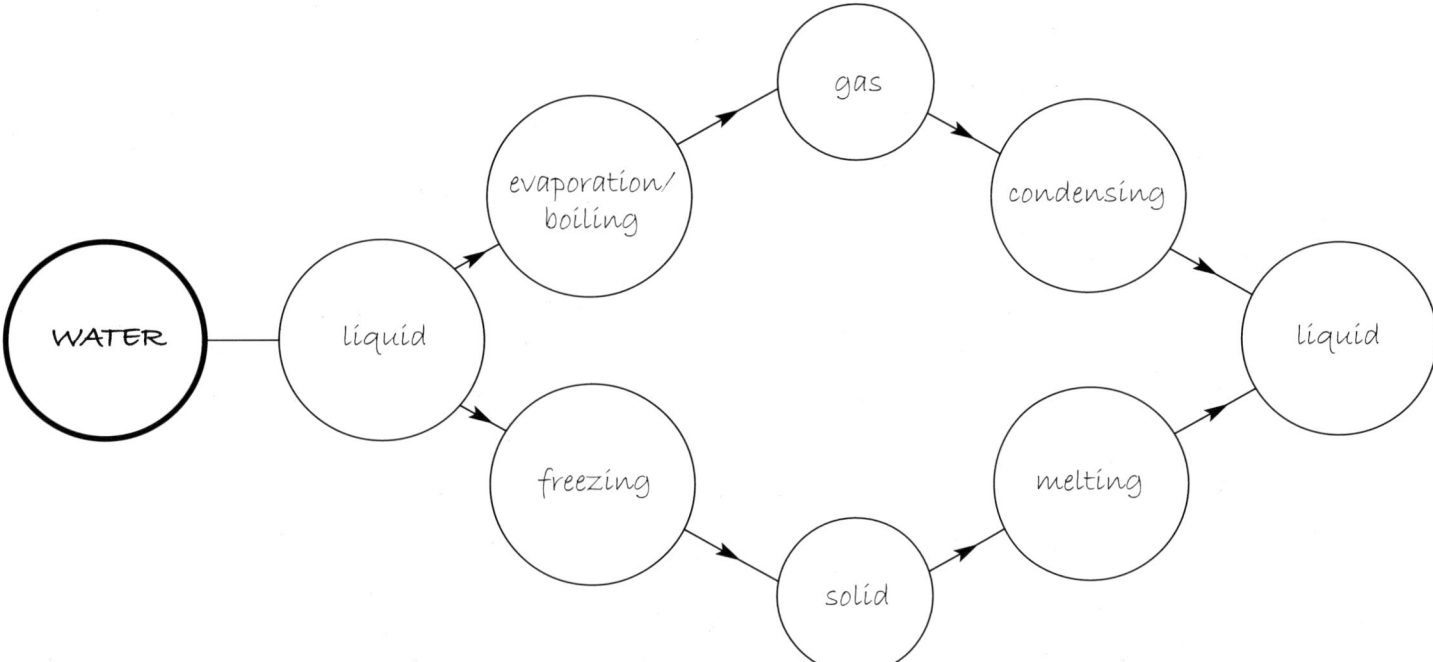

Teaching pupils to read and write persuasion text

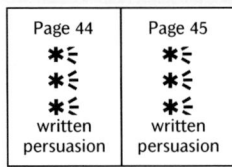

Reading a persuasion text

Read pp 44–45 of *Changing State* pupils' book with the pupils. You will need:

- the written persuasion on pp 44–45 (the text-only version on p 45 of these notes can be enlarged/photocopied/made into an OHT for annotation);
- p 44 of these notes enlarged/photocopied/made into an OHT for annotation.

> SHARED READING ACTIVITY

Audience and purpose

Talk about how the intended audience and purpose affect the language and layout of these pages.

Audience – pupils living in a technologically advanced society.

Purpose – to persuade them that the fate of the world is in their hands.

> SHARED WRITING ACTIVITY

Content and organization

Demonstrate to the pupils how the content of this persuasion text is organized by showing it as a persuasive skeleton – series of bullet points. (See p 47 of these notes.)

> SHARED READING ACTIVITY

Language features and style

Return to the text and talk about the way language features have been used to achieve the effects the author intended. (See annotated example on p 46 of these notes.)

Important features for the pupils' own writing include:

- may be personal or impersonal;
- should be written in the present tense;
- use of emotional language;
- words and phrases that help the author to argue the case by linking causes with their effects.

Explore with the pupils these key concepts:

> INDEPENDENT ACTIVITY

- the ability to write a commentary on an issue setting out and justifying a personal view;
- the ability to construct an argument in note form to persuade others of a point of view and to present the case to the class or a group;
- investigate use of persuasive devices. e.g. 'surely…' 'It wouldn't be difficult…' 'Every right thinking person…'

Challenge the pupils to use the skeleton as the basis of a radio or television advert that highlights the dangers of global warming.

Ask them to draft their views on the issue using the language features set out on p 44 of these notes. Once they have created the script for their advert ask them to reduce it, through note taking, to a series of short paragraphs that they can use as prompts when delivering their persuasive speeches to the class.

© OUP: This page may be reproduced for use solely within the purchaser's school or college

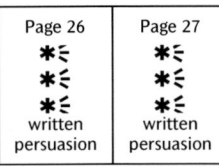

Writing a persuasion text

Use pp 26–27 of *Changing State* pupils' book as a basis for the pupils' own persuasion texts. You will need:

- the written persuasion on pp 26–27;
- p 44 of these notes enlarged/photocopied/made into an OHT for annotation.

SHARED READING ACTIVITY

Content and organization

Revise the content and organization of the persuasion text from the previous session. (See p 47 of this book).

Divide the pupils into pairs. Each pair is going to develop a piece of persuasive writing that they will write in the form of a letter.

PAIRED READING AND WRITING ACTIVITY

The letter is addressed to a petrol company, setting out the dangers of global warming and asking them how they are intending to address these problems.

Before the pupils start writing, read through pp 26–27, marking where the author:

- introduces the argument;
- states the main points;
- elaborates on these points;
- sums up the argument.

Acting as scribe ask the pupils for their ideas as to how they might begin the letter, e.g.

Dear Sir or Madam,

Global warming affects us all: rich and poor, East and West, children and adults alike. We would like to know how you, the suppliers of the petrol that creates much of the exhaust gases, are intending to approach this problem.

Our key points are these:

Language features and style

Remind the pupils of the language features of persuasion texts (see p 44 of these notes).

Audience and purpose

Make clear to the children that they have to try and convince the petrol company through the power of their argument, and that the way they structure it may well have a greater impact than the actual content!

INDEPENDENT WRITING ACTIVITY

Ask the pupils to complete the letter.

© OUP: This page may be reproduced for use solely within the purchaser's school or college

About persuasion text

Audience and purpose

Audience – someone you want to persuade, but who may not know much about the subject.

Purpose – to argue the case for a point of view, persuade someone to buy something or support a cause.

> Sometimes you may know more about the age or interests of your reader

Content and organization

- usually starts with a sentence or paragraph to **introduce the argument**
- the argument is then split into a number of **main points,** each of which probably needs some **elaboration**
- **concluding sentence or paragraph** sums up the argument

> You may have to introduce some important words or ideas the reader needs to know

> The elaboration could be
> – reasons for agreeing with the point
> – examples to back it up
> – further information to explain it.

Language features

- writing may be personal (**first and second person**) or impersonal (**third person**)
- written in the **present tense**
- language may be quite **emotional**, more like a story than other non-fiction
- there may be **rhetorical questions,** which do not really expect an answer
- words and devices showing **cause and effect,** used to **argue** the case
- words and devices that show **movement from one point to the next**

> Use powerful verbs and adjectives, exaggerations or repetition to make an effect

> Is this really important?

> Therefore..., Consequently..., This means that...

> Firstly..., Another reason that..., Thirdly...

The basic skeleton for making notes is pronged bullet points

An example of persuasion text

Stop global warning!

What's the cause?
The greenhouse effect causes global warming. Carbon dioxide and other greenhouse gases trap the Sun's heat in the atmosphere. Greenhouse gases released by burning coal, oil and gas in power stations and vehicles are increasing the global greenhouse effect. The more energy we use, the more greenhouse gases we release.

Research shows that the rising temperatures are linked to increasing human energy consumption.

What are the consequences?
If global warming continues at its present rate droughts and crop failures will become more and more frequent in Africa. Deserts will spread. Millions will starve. Enormous quantities of ice will melt at the poles. Sea levels will rise. Coastal communities around the world will be devastated by floods.

What can you do?
Conserve energy. Do not leave lights burning or travel by car when you can walk or cycle.

Use energy efficiently. Make sure your school and home are well insulated. Don't fill the kettle to the brim to make one cup of coffee.

Find out about alternative energy sources. Solar panels and wind generators do not produce greenhouse gases.

Ask local politicians to explain what they are doing about global warming. How are they making it easier for local people to conserve energy?

Act now!
Tomorrow it will be too late!

Language features and style of persuasion text

Stop global warning!

What's the cause?

The greenhouse effect causes global warming. [Introducing the argument] Carbon dioxide and other greenhouse gases trap the Sun's heat in the atmosphere. [Key terms explained in Glossary] Greenhouse gases released by burning coal, oil and gas in power stations and vehicles are increasing the global greenhouse effect. The more energy we use, the more greenhouse gases we release. [A main point is elaborated]

Research shows that the rising temperatures are linked to increasing human energy consumption.

What are the consequences?

If global warming continues at its present rate droughts and crop failures will become more and more frequent in Africa. Deserts will spread. Millions will starve. Enormous quantities of ice will melt at the poles. Sea levels will rise. Coastal communities around the world will be devastated by floods. [Present tense used throughout] [Causal language] [Emotive language]

What can you do?

Conserve energy. Do not leave lights burning or travel by car when you can walk or cycle.

Use energy efficiently. Make sure your school and home are well insulated. Don't fill the kettle to the brim to make one cup of coffee. [The reader is addressed personally]

Find out about alternative energy sources. Solar panels and wind generators do not produce greenhouse gases. [Movement from one point to the next. (Done, in this case, not by connectives, but by the use of imperatives).]

Ask local politicians to explain what they are doing about global warming. How are they making it easier for local people to conserve energy?

Act now!
Tomorrow it will be too late! [Emotive language]

© OUP: This page may be reproduced for use solely within the purchaser's school or college

If you are using this text with other year groups then also highlight these features:

Y3/P4 ◆ Using the terms singular and plural appropriately.
Y4/P5 ◆ Investigating how style and vocabulary are used to convince the intended reader.
Y6/P7 ◆ Recognizing how arguments are constructed to be effective (e.g. through the provision of persuasive examples).

Content and organization of persuasion text

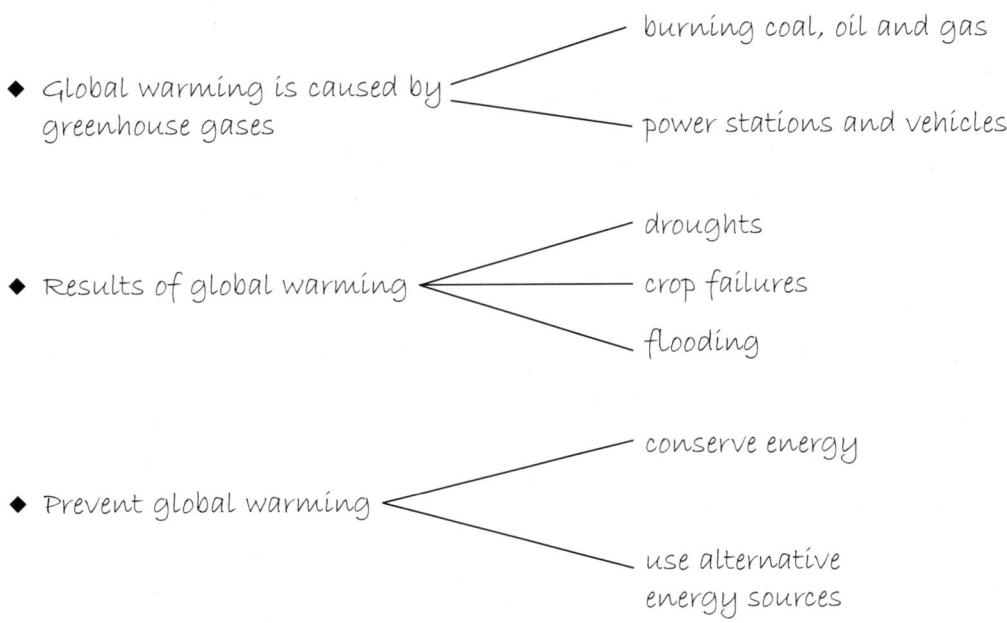

- Global warming is caused by greenhouse gases
  - burning coal, oil and gas
  - power stations and vehicles

- Results of global warming
  - droughts
  - crop failures
  - flooding

- Prevent global warming
  - conserve energy
  - use alternative energy sources

Page	Contents	Text type	National Literacy Strategy Objectives	QCA Science Objectives Unit 5D
				Children should learn:
2	Concept map Contents	Reference	T2 TL 17	
4	Solid, liquid or gas?	Written and visual report	T2 TL 15, 16, 19, 22, 23, 24 T2 SL 5 T2 WL 9	• that materials can be classified as solids, liquids and gases
6	Changing state	Written and visual explanation	T2 TL 15, 16, 19, 22, 23, 24 T2 WL 9	• to know the terms 'melting and 'freezing'
8	What's the temperature?	Written explanation	T2 TL 15, 16, 21 T2 WL 9	• to use a thermometer accurately
10	How thermometers work	Visual explanation	T2 TL 15, 16, 17, 19, 20	
12	Making and using thermometers	Written and visual instructions	T1 TL 22, 25 T1 SL 2, 3, 9	
14	Investigating evaporation	Written and visual recount	T1 TL 21, 23, 25, 26, 27 T1 SL 4	• that evaporation is when a liquid turns to a gas • to explain 'disappearance' of water in a range of situations as evaporation • to explain everyday examples of drying
16	Drying off	Written and visual explanation	T2 TL 15, 16, 17, 20, 21 T2 WL 9	
18	Camp cooler	Written and visual explanation	T2 TL 15, 16, 17, 21 T2 WL 9 T1 TL 22, 25, 26	• to obtain evidence by making careful observations
20	The importance of evaporation	Visual report	T2 TL 16, 22 T2 SL 3, 5, 6 T2 WL 9	• that liquids other than water evaporate
22	Evaporation hazards	Written explanation	T2 TL 15, 16, 17, 20, 21 T2 WL 9	• that liquids other than water evaporate
24	Condensation	Written and visual explanation	T2 TL 15, 16, 17, 20, 21 T2 SL 5, 9 T2 WL 9	• that condensation is when a gas turns to a liquid • that condensation is the reverse of evaporation • that air contains water vapour and when this hits a cold surface it may condense
26	Concerning the damp patches…	Written persuasion	T3 TL 12, 14, 15, 17, 19	
28	Investigating boiling	Written and visual recount	T1 TL 21, 23, 24	• that the boiling temperature of water is 100 °C • to identify patterns in data and use these to make predictions
30	Investigating melting	Written explanation and visual instructions	T2 TL 15, 16, 17, 20, 21 T2 WL 9 T1 TL 22, 25	• to turn ideas into a form that can be investigated, to make a prediction and decide what evidence to collect
32	Melting and boiling points	Written and visual report	T2 TL 16, 20, 22 T2 SL 5, 6	• that melting, freezing, condensing and evaporating are all changes of state which can be reversed
34	Apollo 13	Written and visual recount	T1 TL 21, 23, 24 T1 SL 1, 2, 3	• that liquids other than water evaporate
36	Space disaster	Visual recount	T1 TL 18, 20, 21, 23, 24, 26, 27 T3 TL 3, 7 T1 SL 3, 4, 5	• to obtain evidence by making careful observations
38	Reversible and permanent changes	Written and visual report	T2 TL 16, 20, 22 T2 SL 5	• that melting, freezing, condensing and evaporating are all changes of state which can be reversed
40	Making candles	Written recount and explanation, and visual instructions	T1 TL 22, 24, 25 T1 SL 2, 3, 9	• that evaporation is when a liquid turns to a gas
42	Water cycle	Written and visual explanation	T2 TL 15, 16, 17, 20, 21 T2 SL 5 T2 WL 9	• that water evaporates from oceans, seas and lakes, condenses as clouds and eventually falls as rain • that water collects in streams and rivers and eventually finds its way to the sea • that evaporation and condensation are processes that can be reversed • to interpret the water cycle in terms of the processes involved
44	Time for action!	Written persuasion	T3 TL 13, 14, 15, 16, 17, 18, 19 T3 SL 4, 6, 7	
46	Glossary	Reference	T2 TL 17, 18	
46	Bibliography	Reference	T2 TL 17	
47	Index	Reference	T2 TL 17	

© OUP: This page may be reproduced for use solely within the purchaser's school or college